page 7

page 5

page 6

PHOTOS

Passport Approved

Cost £2.50

You must have the correct amount.
This machine will not accept
1p or 2p coins.

Follow these instructions:

1. Sit down.
2. Adjust seat to the correct height.
3. Pose for the picture.
4. Wait for the red light.
5. Collect photos from outside the booth.

NORTH STREET SHORT-STAY

P CAR PARK
PAY AND DISPLAY

Charges:

Up to 1 hour   30p
1–2 hours   60p
2 hours maximum stay

Charges apply Monday to Saturday
6.00 a.m. to 6.00 p.m.

Car park regulations

Vehicles must be parked only in the marked bays. A valid ticket must be clearly displayed for inspection. Overnight parking is not permitted. Drivers not complying with these regulations will be liable to a fine not exceeding £30.

WELCOME TO MIDDLECASTER'S NEW SHOPPING ARCADE

How To Find Us:

Park in the main car park.
Cross the road and walk through
Puddle Lane to the High Street.
When you reach the signpost turn right.

YOU CAN'T MISS US!
LOTS of NEW SHOPS!

Mr Feet is located just by the entrance.
Can you resist the wonderful smell from
Cathy's Cakes on the opposite side?
His'n'Her Hair is next to Mr Feet.

SPECIAL OFFERS
Car park cost refunded if
you visit the EAT-ME Café.
Two for the price of one on
selected cakes at Cathy's.
Money-off vouchers for CDs
at Funky Music.

WILLIAM SAMPSON
1836–1902

MAYOR OF MIDDLECASTER
1880–1894

Became Sir William in 1892.

Sir William was an important business man. He gave money for many charitable projects in the town. He founded the library and built the Town Hall. He is remembered with great affection by the people of Middlecaster.

On the Notice Board

MIDDLECASTER LEISURE CENTRE

What's on

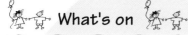

Swimming:

Parents and Toddlers
Tues and Wed 11.00 am
to 12.00 noon

Swimming Classes:

under 8	Mon 4.00 pm to 5.00 pm
8–11	Tues 4.00 pm to 5.00 pm
11–16	Thurs 5.00 pm to 6.00 pm
Adults	Wed 7.00 pm to 9.00 pm
	Fri 8.30 am to 10.30 am

Gymnastics:

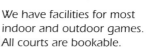

Every Saturday morning
9.00 'til 12.00 noon.

Two groups:
8–10 years
and
11–13 years.

We have facilities for most
indoor and outdoor games.
All courts are bookable.

Ring for a brochure on
02461 582940
or visit our web-site at
www.middleleisure.sporty.uk

FOR SALE

Girl's Bike £50
Suitable for 9 to 11 year old.
Red. Good condition.
With bell and pump.
Only two years old.
One careful owner.

A real bargain.

Also cycle helmet and gloves £10
Please ring 02461 564379
after 6.00 p.m.

FOUND!

On Tuesday evening in
Roseway Crescent

Black kitten – very friendly
Likes to play and eats a lot!
Gets on well with our dog.

Now staying with the Smith
family at 32, Bluebell Crescent.
Please call any time if you think
it might be yours.

Will be sent to the
RSPCA if not claimed
within a week.

Z Z Z z z

Caroline, aged 16,
available for baby sitting.
Most nights.
Good rates.

I am at college, studying child
care, and am very responsible.
I have two younger sisters so
lots of experience!

Please phone 02461 568723
between 12.00 noon and 1.00 p.m.
or between 4.30 and 6.30 p.m.

UNDER 11 FOOTBALL

Boys and **Girls** teams –
All Welcome

Training Sessions –
every Tuesday
at the school at
half past three

Please come – bring
a friend – or ring
Mr Smith on 02461 560032
any evening before 9.00 pm.

Parents welcome too – we need
volunteers to:
  wash the kit
  help with transport
  be supporters!

FOR SALE

Girl's Bike £50
Suitable for 9 to 11 year old.
Red. Good condition.
With bell and pump.
Only two years old.
One careful owner.

A real bargain.

Also cycle helmet and gloves £10
Please ring 02461 564379
after 6.00 p.m.

FOUND!

On Tuesday evening in
Roseway Crescent.

Black kitten – very friendly
Likes to play and eats a lot!
Gets on well with our dog.

Now staying with the Smith
family at 32, Bluebell Crescent.
Please call any time if you think it
might be yours.

Will be sent to the RSPCA if not
claimed within a week.

Baby Sitting

Caroline, aged 16,
available for baby sitting.
Most nights.
Good rates.

I am at college, studying child care, and am very responsible. I have two younger sisters so lots of experience!

Please phone 02461 568723
between 12.00 noon and 1.00 p.m. or between 4.30 and 6.30 p.m.

Caroline, aged 16,
available for baby sitting.
Most nights.
Good rates.

I am at college, studying child care, and am very responsible. I have two younger sisters so lots of experience!

Please phone 02461 568723
between 12.00 noon and 1.00 p.m. or between 4.30 and 6.30 p.m.

Under 11 Football

Boys and Girls teams –
All Welcome

Training Sessions –
every Tuesday
at the school at half past three

Please come – bring a friend –
or ring Mr Smith on 02461 560032
any evening before 9.00 p.m.

Parents welcome too – we need
volunteers to:
    wash the kit
    help with transport
    be supporters!

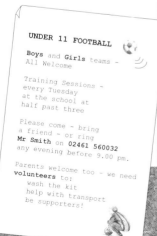

UNDER 11 FOOTBALL

Boys and Girls teams –
All Welcome

Training Sessions –
every Tuesday
at the school at
half past three

Please come – bring
a friend – or ring
Mr Smith on 02461 560032
any evening before 9.00 pm.

Parents welcome too – we need
volunteers to:
    wash the kit
    help with transport
    be supporters!

MIDDLECASTER LEISURE CENTRE

 What's on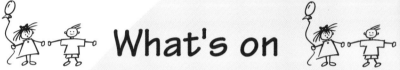

★ **Swimming:**

★ Parents and Toddlers
Tues and Wed 11.00 am
to 12.00 noon

★ Swimming Classes:

under 8	Mon 4.00 pm to 5.00 pm
8–11	Tues 4.00 pm to 5.00 pm
11–16	Thurs 5.00 pm to 6.00 pm
Adults	Wed 7.00 pm to 9.00 pm
	Fri 8.30 am to 10.30 am

✱ Gymnastics:

Every Saturday morning
9.00 'til 12.00 noon.

Two groups:
8–10 years
and
11–13 years.

We have facilities for most
indoor and outdoor games.
All courts are bookable.

Ring for a brochure on
02461 582940
or visit our web-site at
www.middleleisure.sporty.uk

page 18–19

page 23

page 22

page 20—21

USING YOUR MICROWAVE

In the Kitchen

New Fruity Snaps
The anytime, anywhere, anyplace cereal.

Not just for breakfast – take a handful for lunch – a bowlful for supper!

A new sensation for your mouth!

High in fibre – low in fat.

Lots of lovely vitamins!

New Fruity Snaps

The anytime, anywhere, anyplace cereal.

Contents:

crunchy flakes of wheat and bran, dried fruit selection de-luxe – apples, bananas and apricots, with added raisins and nuts.

SAFETY FIRST

DO NOT tamper with the door – microwave energy can harm you.

DO NOT overcook – some foods may ignite.

DO NOT stir heated liquids immediately – delayed eruptive boiling may occur.

DO NOT operate if damaged – repairs must be undertaken by a qualified engineer.

Ring our help-line on 012345 987652 or e-mail us at magicmicros@cookin.co.uk

USING YOUR MICROWAVE OVEN

Display Window

Tells you which function is selected.

Cooking Time

Current time display when the appliance
is not in use.

Defrost

Sets defrosting time.

Ready Meals

Does the work for you.
Look at the lists and choose the setting.

Time

Press here to set your own
cooking time.
Press number pads to set how long –
in seconds.

Start

Press to begin cooking.

Kids

Have had to go round to Gran's.
Everything O.K. – Don't worry.

Will be back about 6.

Dinner is in the fridge. Heat
each on Ready Meals setting 4.
Take care when you take the
plates out.

There are some sweetie bars
in the tin or you can have some
Fruity Snaps.

Make a start on
your homework.

　See you soon

　　Mum

　　xxx

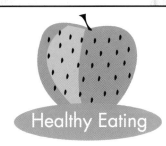

Healthy Eating

Two things to watch out for are sugar and salt.

Many products use lots of both of these but the packaging doesn't tell you!

Your body needs some salt but salt levels in processed foods are often too high.

Choose foods with natural sugar – like fresh fruit.

Middlecas

New Shopping arcade opens

Forest Flowers
10% off delivery for first week

Residents protest

Coupo...

Local Hero

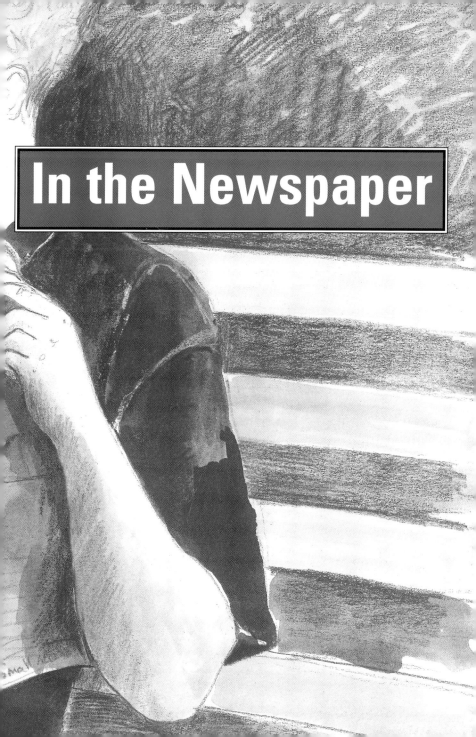

In the Newspaper

WHAT'S ON THIS WEEK

The Leisure Centre begins the new season's **swimming sessions** from Monday. Check their leaflets for days and times.

Auditions for Middlecaster **Amateur Dramatic Society** will be at the Community Centre from 7.30 on Wednesday and Thursday nights.

The **Youth Club Dance** will be on Friday.

Middlecaster Primary School's **Autumn Fête** is this Saturday. (On the field if fine or in the school hall if wet.)

WHAT'S ON THIS WEEK

- The Leisure Centre begins the new season's **swimming sessions** from Monday. Check their leaflets for days and times.

- Auditions for Middlecaster **Amateur Dramatic Society** will be at the Community Centre from 7.30 on Wednesday and Thursday night.

- The **Youth Club Dance** will be on Friday.

- Middlecaster Primary School's **Autumn Fête** is this Saturday. (On the field if fine or in the school hall if wet.)

26

First class raid

Leanne Stevens was highly praised by local police after her part in helping to track down three post-office raiders last week.

Leanne was standing outside the post office when two men ran out. They jumped into a waiting car and were driven off by a third man.

Quick-witted Leanne noted the car number and told the police straight away. The car was stopped within half an hour.

First class raid

Leanne Stevens was highly praised by local police after her part in helping to track down three post-office raiders last week.

Leanne was standing outside the post office when two men ran out. They jumped into a waiting car and were driven off by a third man.

Quick-witted Leanne noted the car number and told the police straight away. The car was stopped within half an hour.

Lost on Monday

Small black **kitten** with white patch under chin. Answers to the name of Lucky. Very friendly. Reward offered to finder.

Please ring 02461 569938 any time.

FOR SALE

● F-reg Ford
Vgc. MOT and service history.
£850 ono.
Contact Phil on
02461 836792 for test drive.

CAMPAIGN AGAINST LOCAL SHOPPING CENTRE

THIS WEEK saw the opening of the new shopping centre. There has been a long campaign on the part of some residents and local shopkeepers against the shopping centre.

Fears have been expressed that the centre will damage trade for many of the local shops. Many of the residents have signed a petition which claimed 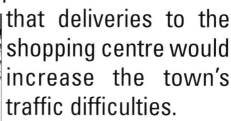 that deliveries to the shopping centre would increase the town's traffic difficulties.

Mrs Jones, who has played a leading rôle in the campaign, said at a recent meeting in the town hall that the council had taken no notice of the protests. She stated that there are a lot of people who are very unhappy about the situation and called on local residents to boycott the new centre.

The manager of Sampson's Supermarket, Ms Gill Friend and Bob Phillips, the owner of the corner shop have spearheaded the local traders' protest group. Ms Friend, speaking for the group, applauded Mrs Jones's call for a boycott. 'There is not

enough trade in the town to make it possible to support all these new businesses,' she says.

A spokesman for the company behind the shopping-centre project denied that there had been any pressure put on the local council. He did agree that the company had agreed to contribute a substantial sum of money for local projects. 'We are not in competition with existing business,' he said. 'We aim to offer local people the sort of facilities and choice they would expect to see in any growing town.'

The debate seems set to continue.

Dahlia Drive,
Middlecaster

Dear Sir,

I think that the opening of the new shopping arcade is a very bad thing. Middlecaster likes its little local shops. We don't want to lose these because big firms move in.

I also think that we have enough traffic problems in the town anyway. We don't need any more delivery lorries blocking the streets.

Yours faithfully,

Mrs M. Jones